Oozing with Slime fun!

NICKELODEON SLIME: ANNUAL 2019

A CENTUM BOOK 978-1-912707-12-6

Published in Great Britain by Centum Books Ltd
This edition published 2018

1 3 5 7 9 10 8 6 4 2

Centum Books Ltd, 20 Devon Square, Newton Abbot, Devon, TQ12 2HR, UK
books@centumbooksltd.co.uk

CENTUM BOOKS Limited Reg. No. 07641486

Slime bubble image p34 © Lorraine Teigland

A CIP catalogue record for this book is available from the British Library.

Printed in Italy

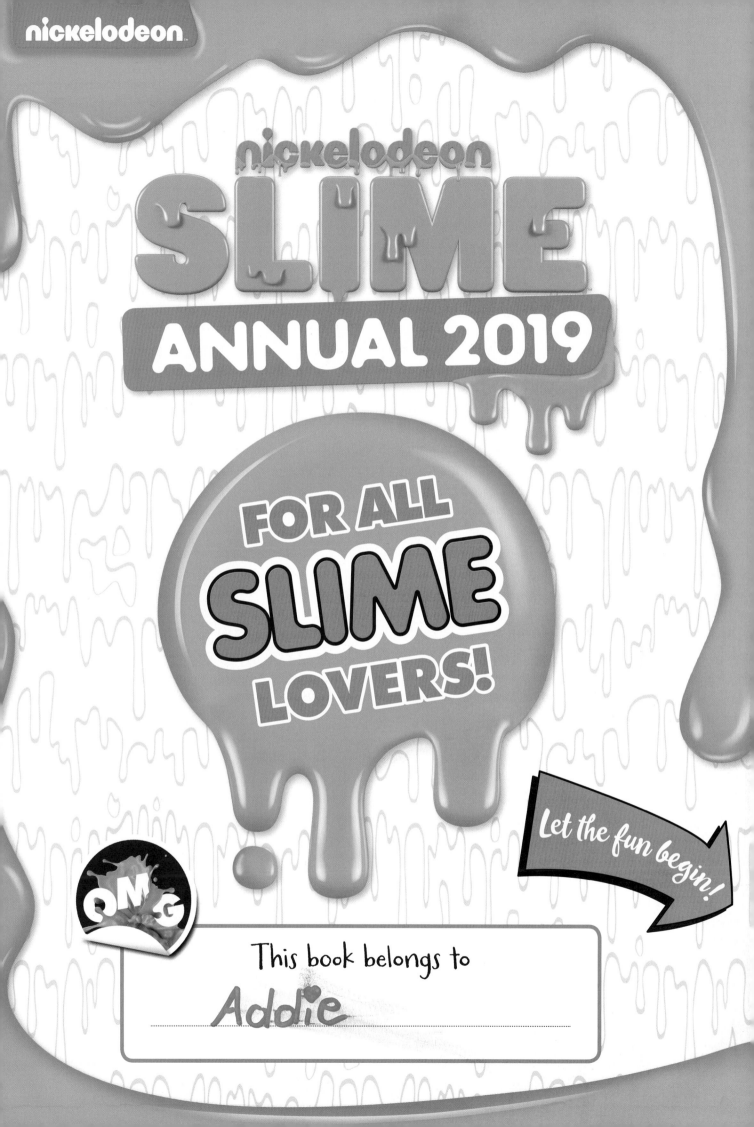

Contents

SLIME FACTS!

Slime has been oozing around for a long time. There are countless different recipes for it and it has given loads of kids awesome, fun Slime times. You can even go to Nickelodeon SlimeFes – a day devoted to Slime-filled pranks!

1

Nickelodeon SlimeFest started in Australia in **2012.**

2

Q: What year was Justin Bieber Slimed at the Kids' Choice Awards?

A: 2012

3

Q: When did JoJo Siwa get Slimed at the Kids' Choice Awards in 2018?

A: At the end of her set, after singing all her hits!

4

The world's biggest Slime was created in New York by Maddie Rae in 2017. Hundreds of kids helped to make it!

5

The first time green Slime appeared on television was in 1979 on a Canadian show called *You Can't Do That on Television.*

6

SlimeFest is now an annual event in Spain, Italy and the UK.

7

Q: Who out of these two celebrities has been Slimed the most at the Kids' Choice Awards: Jack Black or Jim Carrey?

A: Jack Black!

Historical SLIME

This may not be true!

Slime was discovered by the Romans in 40BC when a child mixed some cornflour and water and left the Slimy substance outside. A soldier slid on some and ended up slipping all over the place. To stop this ever happening again the Romans invented straight lines, hence the term 'straight as a Roman road!'

WHOOPS

There was a time in **Ancient Eygpt** when Slime was seen dripping from the Sphinx's nose.

The Aztecs used Slime to warn off their enemies. They would lay in wait and throw it off the top of their famous statues!

Count the number of times you can find the word Slime on these two pages!

If you believed all that... you should get **Slimed!**

Answer on page **92**.

Basic SLIME RECIPES!

Make Your Own Slime!

This can form the base for lots of different and exciting Slime.

You will need:
- [ ] 1 cup PVA glue
- [ ] 1 tsp bicarbonate of soda
- [ ] Food colouring or liquid watercolour paint
- [ ] 2 tsps eyewash (it must contain boric acid and sodium borate)

GLUE

1 Combine the glue and the bicarbonate of soda – mix very well.

2 Colour using food colouring or liquid watercolour paint and add whatever you fancy.

3 Now add the eyewash and bring it together – it should be turning into Slime!

Warning!
Make sure you ask an adult before making this and if you use food colouring be aware it can stain.

TOP TIP
Once you know how to make it, you can create any kind of Slime you can dream up!

Pimp Your SLIME!

Here are some fun ideas to take your Slime to the next level!

Flowers

Gems

Sand

Sequins

Glitter

Paints

Pom Poms

Small Toys

Beads

Food Colouring

LAUGH OUT LOUD!

What's the worst thing about being an Octopus?

ANSWER: Washing your hands after making Slime!

Gross SLIME Facts

An elephant bogie is the ultimate Slime ball – it's the size of a

basketball!

Which would you prefer to sneeze out?!

PAAARP!

From Ancient Greece to the Middle Ages snail Slime was used in cough syrup!

OMG

GULP!

CURES ALL

Camels can Slime you with their spit – it's a mixture of stomach juice and saliva!

YOU GOT SLIMED GOOD!

12

More SLIME! WORDSEARCH

How many times can you find the word SLIME in this wordsearch?

It's forwards, backwards, up, down and all other ways you can imagine!

S S E I L E M I L S
S S L I L I M E E L E M L
L L I S I S M I S I
I I M L E M L L I M
M M E E M I L S M L E
E E M I L S E M I L S
S S L I M E S L I M E
E M I L S S L I M E I
I S L I M E M I L S
L E M I L S L I M E

Slime Snot!

Make this amazing Slime snot. It really does look likes snot – gross!

You will need:
- [ ] Shampoo
- [ ] Green food colouring
- [ ] Sea salt

Warning!
Make sure you ask an adult before making this and be aware that food colouring can stain.

1 Put a small amount of shampoo – preferably white, in a bowl.

GREEN!

Warning!
Don't actually put this on your nose!

2 Colour using green food colouring.

If it's not coming together you can add some talcum powder!

3 Add a pinch of sea salt and stir until it all comes together in a perfect Slime consistency.

14

Top 5 Ways to Prank Your Friends with Slime Snot!

1

Pretend to **pick** your **nose** and then pull a ball of Slime out and start **playing** with it.

EWWW!

2

Open your **lunchbox**, pretend to sneeze and then find the **Slimy** snot that's landed on your **lunch!**

Vlog it!

This one would work well as a vlog!

3

Pretend to **sneeze** into a tissue and have the **Slime snot** ready to open up and gross out your **friends.**

OMG

4

Pretend to splash some Slime on your friend's purse or **pencil case** and watch them *scream!*

5

Pretend to sneeze into a glass of water, **drop** the Slime in and **offer** your friend a drink!

GROSS!

YUCK!

SLIME RECIPES!

Gigantic MULTICOLOURED Slime!

You'll want to make a lot of Slime for this so you can have loads of fun using all the different colours together!

For each Slime you will need:

☐ 1 cup PVA glue

☐ 1 tsp bicarbonate of soda

☐ 2 tsps eyewash (it must contain boric acid and sodium borate)

☐ Food colouring or paint

Warning!
Make sure you ask an adult before making this and if you use food colouring be aware it can stain.

GLUE

To make a big batch just DOUBLE or TREBLE the recipe!

1 Combine the glue and the bicarbonate of soda – mix very well.

2 Now add the eyewash and bring it together – it should be turning into Slime!

3 You can either mix up a big batch and then separate to colour or decorate, or just mix up smaller batches.

4 Colour using food colouring in pink, blue, yellow and purple – pretty!

5 Play!

Ideas for your Multicoloured Slime

Mix it!

Mix it and see how long it takes for the colours to blend.

Be very organised and put it all into separate containers.

Ooh! Get you!

Plait it!

Sort it!

Colour it!

Make it into a Rainbow!

Twist it!

17

SLIME!
Doodling

Doodle your Slime all over this page.
Take it wherever it wants to go!

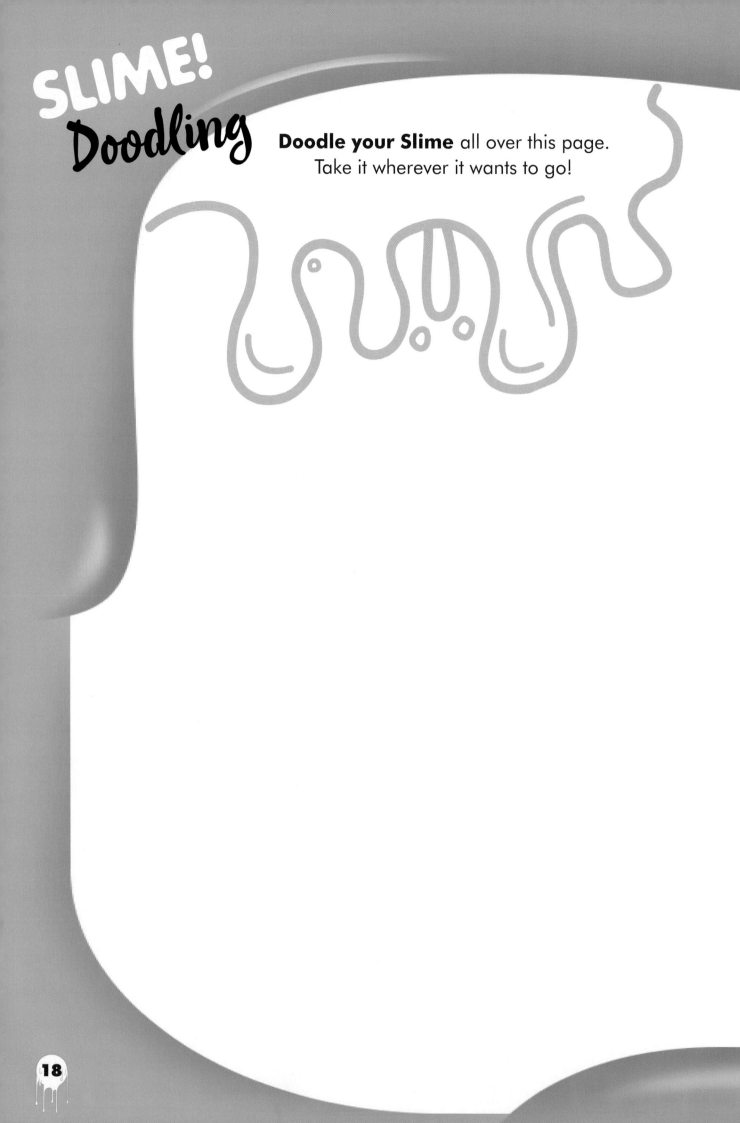

Prank
SLIME PIZZA!

Make a delicious pizza – out of Slime!! Offer your hungry friends a slice and fall about laughing when they try to pick it up!

You will need:

☐ White Slime (for the dough) or a shop-bought pizza base.

☐ Red Slime (for the tomato sauce). That ketchup Slime from page 28 might come in handy here!

☐ Yellow Slime (for the cheese).

☐ Toppings – you can use real ones, or plastic toy food ones, or you can try and make them from Slime!

Serve this:

⬤ On a plate
⬤ In a pizza box
⬤ On your hand?!

Warning!
Remember this is just a joke! Don't let anyone really take a bite!

Or get someone to dress up as a pizza delivery guy and drop it off!

Vlog it!

This one would work well as a vlog!

One slice or two?

Double the joke by serving with prank juice from pages **80–81**!

YUCK!

21

IN THE LAB!

1 Slime **stretches** in a most unusual way. Try and stretch Slime quickly – it will break up. Stretch the Slime slowly and it will get longer and longer and longer.

2 Why? It's a non-Newtonian fluid. This means that it behaves like both a solid and a liquid at the same time.

Non-Newtonian fluid

LABTIME

Question

Q Is it a **liquid** or a **solid**?

A Neither! It's SLIME!

3 When you apply PRESSURE, it turns into a solid (so to speak) and breaks apart. When you let Slime flow like a liquid, it stretches with no problem.

22

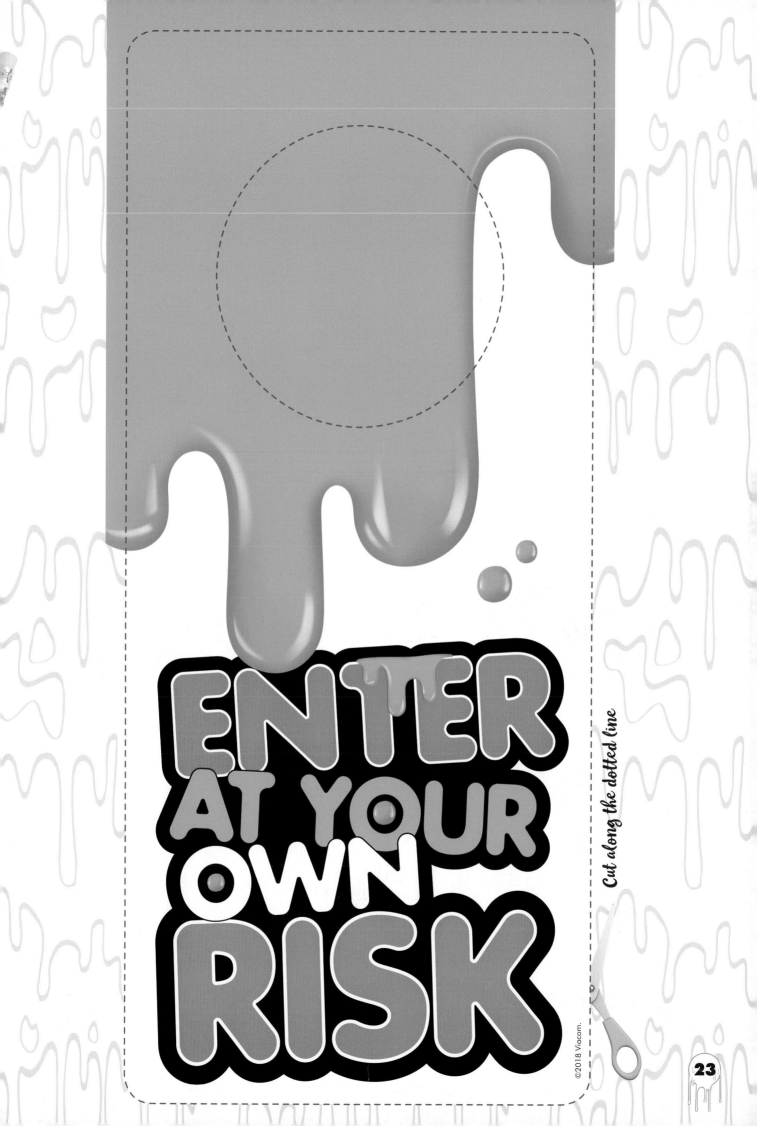

ENTER AT YOUR OWN RISK

Cut along the dotted line

©2018 Viacom.

23

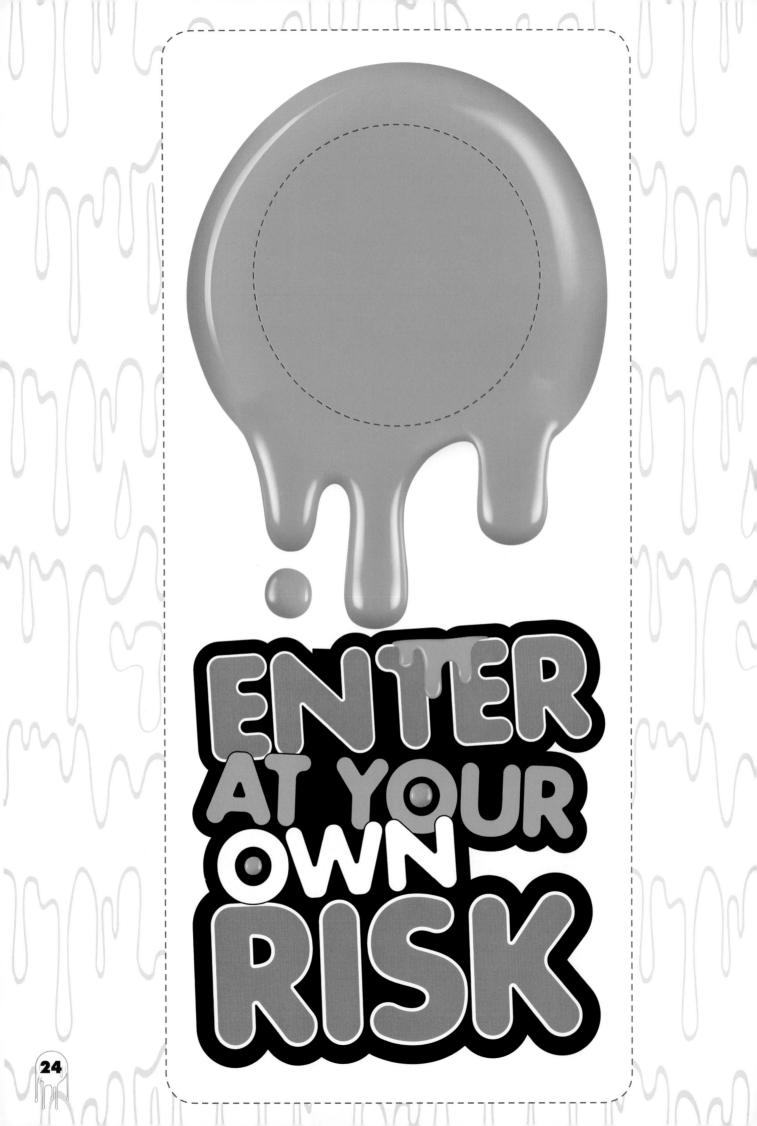

KEEP OUT ...or be SLIMED!

Cut along the dotted line

KEEP OUT ...or be SLIMED!

SLIME!
ANAGRAMS

Circle the words that can be made using the letters in

SLIME

mile, lemon, lime, (slim,) less, smile, silly, elm, semi, like, is, sim, mole, limp, lie, meal, mime, sly, line, me

Answers on page **92**.

Prank
KETCHUP SLIME!

This fake ketchup Slime will shock your friends.

Warning!
Make sure you ask an adult before making this and if you use food colouring be aware it can stain.

1 Mix the water, fibre powder and food colouring together into the empty ketchup bottle.

2 Ask an adult to microwave it for one minute.

01:00

3 It should now have a Slimy consistency.

4 Wait until your friends are asking for ketchup and pass them the ketchup Slime! Hilarious!!

YUCK! YUCK! YUCK!

Warning! It won't taste nice but it's not dangerous to eat.

Vlog it!

This one would work well as a vlog!

POPPING SLIME!

Make this supercool Slime and terrify your friends – tell them it's alive!

GLUE + + +

1 Combine the glue and the bicarbonate of soda – mix very well.

2 Colour using food colouring.

OMG

3 Now add the eyewash and bring it together – it should be turning into Slime!

pop! pop! pop!

4 Next add the popping candy – it will start popping straight away!

5 Play!

IN THE LAB!

Popping candy has carbon dioxide trapped into it when it's made. The sugar is heated under high pressure. When it cools, the carbon dioxide can't escape unless it gets wet.

Sugar

CO_2

As it escapes it...

POP...POP...POPS!

31

SLIME!
Slogans

Make up your own Slime slogans and design them to look like they're dripping with Slime!

It's SLIME Time

BISE AND SLIME

SLIME Bubbles Competition

Make these awesome Slime bubbles using a straw to blow them as **big** as you dare!

How to do it:

1. Make your ball of Slime – use one of the recipes from this book.

2. You'll need a straw!

3. Put the straw into the ball of Slime and blow.

DO NOT SUCK!!

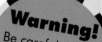

Warning!
Be careful not to suck the Slime through the straw – it's disgusting!

Game ON!

WINNER

You can make this into a game by taking it in turns with a friend to try and pop the bubbles. Whoever can blow the biggest bubble without it being popped wins!

And the winner is...

LABTIME Question

Q Why when you seal them do bubbles always become a sphere?

A Because the tension in the bubble skin shrinks to the smallest possible shape for the volume of air it contains. Compared to any other shape, a sphere has the smallest surface area for the amount of volume.

Yummy Stripy SLIME

You can eat this amazing Slime — *delicious!*

You will need:

- ☐ 2 packets of chewy sweets in 3 different colours (so 6 packets in total)
- ☐ 3 bowls
- ☐ baking paper

This recipe serves 6!

1 Put each colour of chewy sweets into a separate bowl lined with baking paper.

2 Ask an adult to microwave each bowl for 10 seconds (you may need to heat them for 20 seconds, but check them after 10 seconds).

00:10

TOP TIP

Can't find different coloured sweets? Add food colouring before putting in the microwave — just like we've done here:

3 Once they have cooled, lift them out — leave them on the baking paper.

Warning!
Ask an adult to help you with the microwave and check if they have cooled enough.

4 Once they are cool enough to handle roll them into long sausage shapes and then start plaiting!

Don't put it in your hair!

TROUBLESHOOTING!

If you are having problems with your Slime then see if our handy troubleshooter guide might help.

TOO STICKY?

...add a few more drops of eyewash.

GLUE

BREAKING UP?

...maybe you've added too much eyewash? Add some more glue.

GOING HARD?

...it won't last forever – make some more!

NOT WORKING?

...did you use saline solution? This won't work unless it contains sodium borate and boric acid.

Warning!
Don't ever pour your Slime down the drain – it will block it!

NOT MULTICOLOURED ANYMORE?

...the colours will eventually go into a sludge together – you'll just have to make more Slime!

TOP TIP

Make sure you store your Slime correctly – it needs to be in an airtight container. A plastic box with a lid is perfect, or use a ziplock bag.

FLUFFY SLIME!
CODEBREAKER

We have done the first one for you.

The recipe for Fluffy Slime has gone missing. Crack the code to find the crucial ingredient.

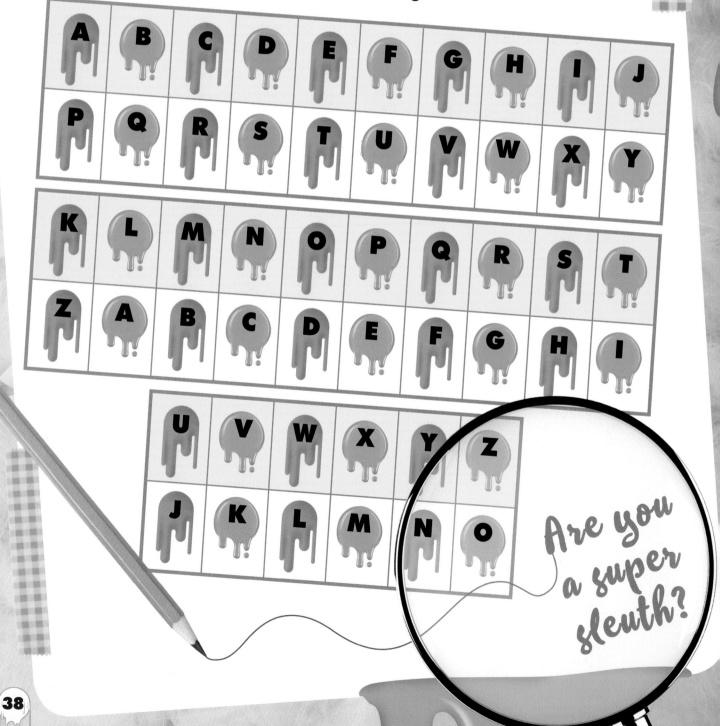

Are you a super sleuth?

DSLGTYR QZLX

SHAVING FOAM

Answer on page **92**.

You will need:

☐ 1 cup PVA glue

☐ 1 tsp bicarbonate of soda

☐ 1-4 cups Shaving foam

☐ 2 tsps eyewash (it must contain boric acid and sodium borate)

1 Combine the glue and the bicarbonate of soda – mix very well.

3 Add the eyewash and bring it together – it should be turning into Slime!

?

2 Now add your mystery ingredient!

TOP TIP
If it gets too sticky you can add a few more drops of the eyewash.

4 PLAY!

IN THE LAB!

LABTIME
Question

Q What happens when you mix Slime?

A The glue with the other ingredients produces a putty-like material that's elastic and flows very slowly.

LABTIME
Question

Q What's a polymer?

A A polymer is a long chain of identical, repeating molecules.

LABTIME
Question

Q What is an atom?

A The smallest part of a chemical element.

LABTIME
Question

Q What's a molecule?

A A molecule is made up of atoms that are held together by chemical bonds.

LABTIME
Question

Q What's glue made of?

A It's a polymer material.

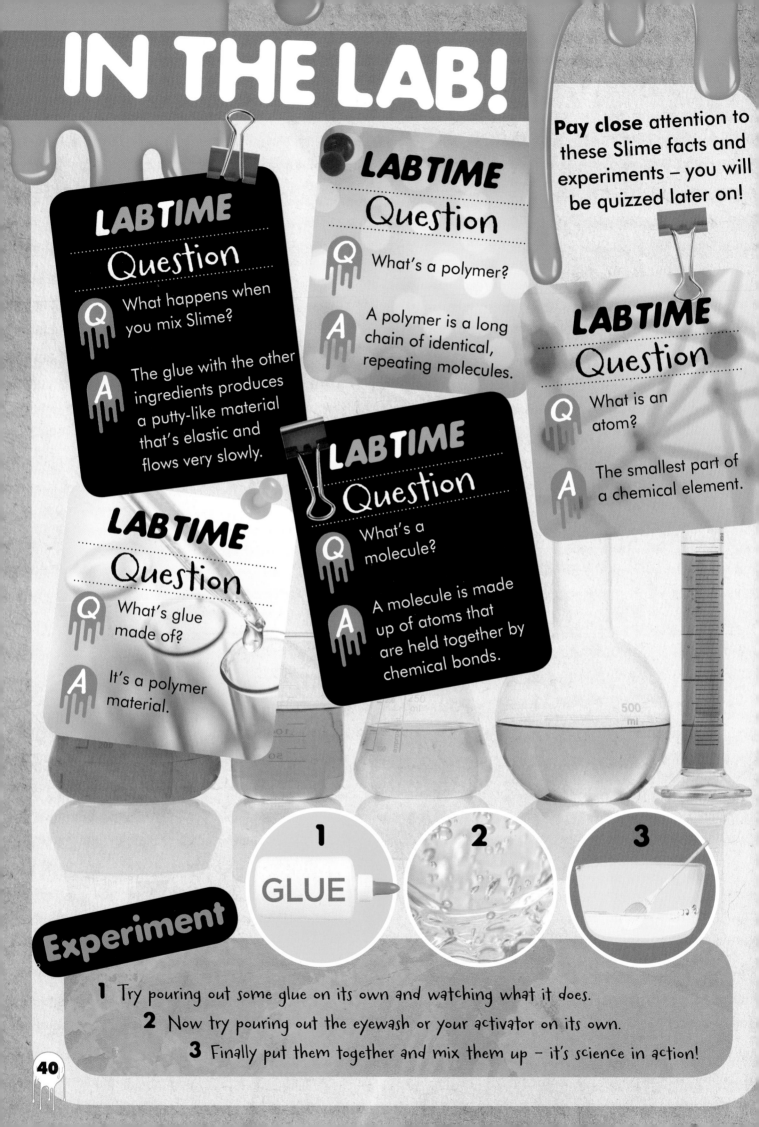

1 GLUE

2

3

Experiment

1 Try pouring out some glue on its own and watching what it does.

2 Now try pouring out the eyewash or your activator on its own.

3 Finally put them together and mix them up – it's science in action!

Here's your **glue** – it's quite thick but it's classified as a liquid.

Here's your **eyewash** or whatever you use to activate your Slime – when you put it with the glue it joins together and starts to solidify. But it still keeps some of its liquid properties.

You can imagine the **polymers** as tiny steel chains, that are all interlinked.

When you add the activator (eyewash or whatever you use) it's like you've added a load of tiny **magnets**. The magnets help the steel chains to all stick together, but it doesn't quite lose its liquid state.

The Slime is linked together in more than one place and that is why it acts more like a solid. This is called **cross-linking.**

Who is Getting SLIMED?

It can be difficult to **choose** which of your besties is going to get lucky with the Slime next. **Here's a fun way** to decide who has the honour!

Write your friends' names in the boxes opposite →

Do they have an **S** in their name? Cross it out!

Do they have an **L** in their name? Cross it out!

Do they have an **I** in their name? Cross it out!

Do they have an **M** in their name? Cross it out!

Do they have an **E** in their name? Cross it out!

The person with the most letters crossed out is the lucky winner!

Your FIVE Friends

1

2

3

4

5

Draw or stick the winner's picture here.

And the winner is...

Write their name here...

WINNER

43

SLIME PARTY

Party time with Slime!

My Slime Party

Dress code:
....
....

Food:
....
....
....

Drinks:
....
....

Games to play:
....
....
....

Guest list:
....
....
....
....
....

44

Warning!
Make sure you ask an adult's permission before inviting everyone!

Design your party invitation here:

Party games and food ideas:

When it's time for food, play the Slime pizza joke from pages 20-21 – don't eat it!

Make some awesome Slime! Whose is the craziest?

Blow Slime bubbles. Whose can get the biggest?

Make up your own bucket of Slime and Slime your guests!

Pop a grape into a friend's mouth and tell them it's an eyeball!

Slime green jelly would make a great dessert!

How about Slime green smoothies?

Underground MAZE

Start

Find your way through the Slime maze to get to the Slime tank before anyone else.

It's A-maze-ing!

Answer on page 92.

OMG

Slime Sequences

Can you work out what's next in these Slime ingredient sequences?

FLUFFY SLIME!

GLITTER SLIME!

POMPOM SLIME!

Answers on page 92.

My SLIME Diary

11 yrs

week

Coolest Slime recipe you've made?

Glitter slime

What's your favourite Slime?

all of them

Wednesday
18

Best Slime prank you've pulled?

None

Who would you most like to Slime?

My Dad

48

How many times have you been Slimed?

0

Worst Slime recipe you've made?
Detergent slime. It gives you a rash.

What Slimes have you made?
- glitter slime
- different coulor slime.

What Slime prank would you like to do?
Door trigen a bucket full of slime to fall on someones head.

Best thing you've added to Slime?
Glitter

Who have you Slimed?
No one.

Find the SLIME

Slime is great at hiding! Use the directions to find it.

50

Answer on page **92**.

Smelly SLIME!

You will need:

☐ 1 cup PVA glue

☐ 1 tsp bicarbonate of soda

☐ Food colouring

☐ Scents – vanilla essence, mint food flavouring, or lavender oil

☐ 2 tsps eyewash (it must contain boric acid and sodium borate)

Warning!
Make sure you check with a grown-up before adding extra ingredients to Slime!

Lavender

Mint

Vanilla

GLUE

1 Combine the glue and the bicarbonate of soda – mix very well.

2 Colour using food colouring and add the scent now.

3 Add the eyewash and bring it together – it should be turning into Slime!

4 Play!

TOP TIP

You can also use smells that are a bit yucky to scent your Slime and then prank people by asking them to smell it. Marmite or soya sauce might work well.

SPOT THE DIFFERENCE

Find the ten differences
between these two pictures.

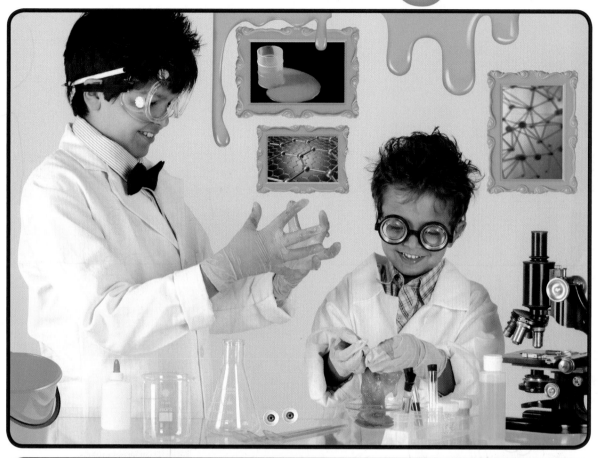

Answers on page **93**.

Name That SLIME!

Fluffy Slime and Glitter Slime may sound fine, but why not dream up some new amazing names for these colourful images? Then stick in and name some of your own creations!

What shall we call this one?

Stick your Slime pic here

Name:

Name:

Stick your Slime pic here

Name:

Name:

54

How about Fantabulist Glittery Glottery Slippery Slime?

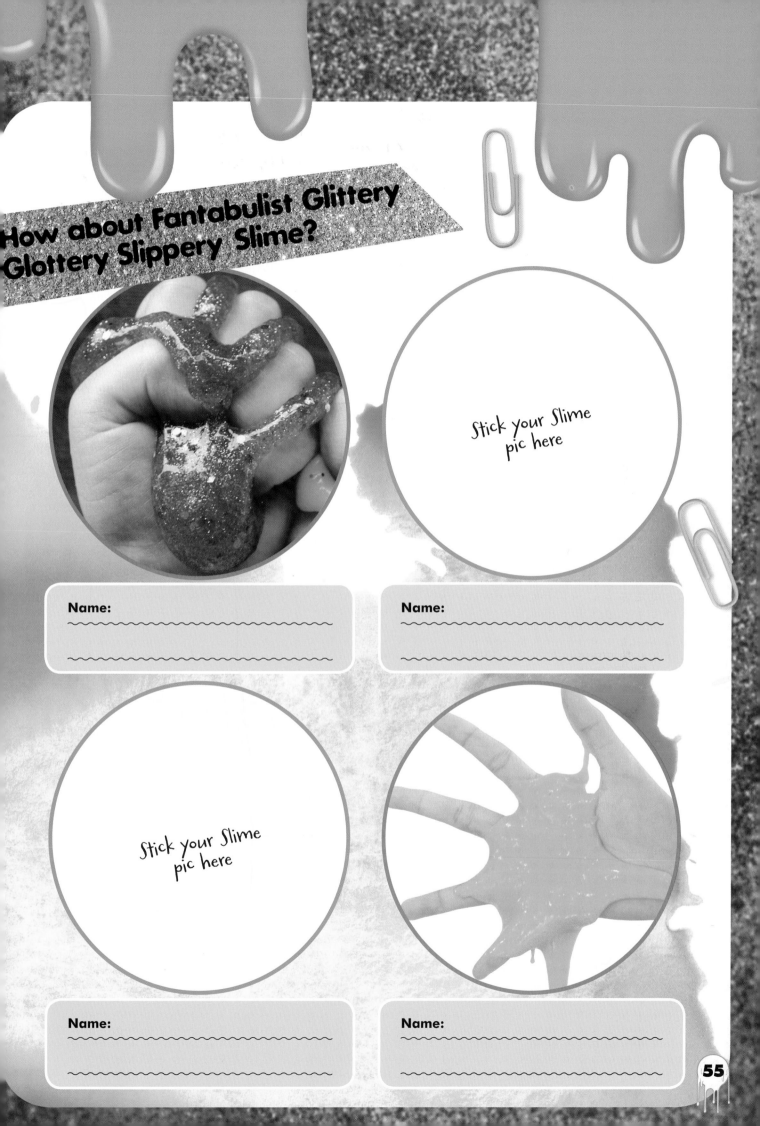

Stick your Slime pic here

Name:

Name:

Stick your Slime pic here

Name:

Name:

All about liquids!

Water (and most other liquids) is made up of little, unconnected molecules that bounce around each other.

These unconnected molecules are called monomers. They are not normally gooey or sticky.

If you have a liquid that is gooey or sticky it's called a polymer. These molecules are linked together and flow more slowly.

Experiment!

1

Take a **bottle** of ketchup and a glass of water.

2

Pour the ketchup into your water. What happens?

3

Now try stirring the liquids together. What happens to them?

Glue – what is it good for?

The glue you use for craft activities and to make Slime is used by the plastics industry to form surface coatings. It's also used to make artificial sponges, hoses and printing inks.

PVA Glue

Experiment!

Smear a bit of your glue onto a hard surface (a plate or something like that will work).

Leave it for a few hours – or a day if you've squeezed out quite a lot!

Smear the glue...

What happens to it?

Make sure you ask a grown-up before using the glue!

Bubbling SWAMP SLIME

You will need:

- [ ] 1 cup PVA glue
- [ ] Green food colouring
- [ ] 1 tsp bicarbonate of soda
- [ ] 2 tsps eyewash (it must contain boric acid and sodium borate)
- [ ] White vinegar

Warning! Don't do this one without a grown-up's permission.

GREEN!

1 Measure out the glue.

2 Colour using green food colouring.

3 Mix in the bicarbonate of soda.

4 Add the eyewash and bring it together – it should be turning into Slime!

5 Now put the Slime in a container and take it outside.

Vlog it!

This one would work well as a vlog!

6 Ask a grown-up to help you pour the white vinegar onto the Slime.

WHITE VINEGAR

7 # Watch it EXPLODE!

TOP TIP

Add in some plastic creatures to make it look like a real bubbling swamp.

Edible
EYEBALL SLIME

You will need:

Allow two eyeballs per person

- ☐ Currants
- ☐ A round ice cube tray mould
- ☐ A packet of blackcurrant jelly
- ☐ Blue food colouring
- ☐ Greek yoghurt (can be flavoured to make it sweeter)

1 Put a currant into each ice cube space – this is your pupil.

2 Mix the blackcurrant jelly with only half the water that it says on the packet (we want it quite solid!) and then add some drops of blue food colouring.

3 Now spoon it into the ice cube tray – about half way.

4 Chill in the fridge until set.

5 Once it's firm take it out and top up with the yoghurt.

6 Put in the freezer for a few hours – overnight is perfect.

7 Once it's all firm, take it out of the fridge, gently turn it upside down and remove each eyeball from the mould. You can run hot water over the bottom of the mould to help loosen them if you wish.

Freak out your friends...

...when you pick up an eyeball and pop it into your mouth.

Yummy, wobbly!

OMG

What do you call Slime with no eyes?

ANSWER: Slime!

61

Draw a scene with people at the bottom of the page and then make the Slime drip slowly down until they are covered!

Make sure you have your best Slime green colour handy!

SLIME OR NOT SLIME?

Gather together some Slimy substances and then get a friend to tell you whether they are Slime or not!

You'll need to blindfold them, otherwise they'll be able to see what they are doing!

Slime

Slime

Jelly Worms

Jam

Jelly

My friend thought it was...

YUCK!
Rating
☐/10

Plasticine

Make sure you wash your hands!

Yoghurt

64

SLIMED SUDOKU!

There must only be one of each Slime in each of the four boxes, columns or rows.

Answer on page **93**.

You'll need to use your colouring pens for this special Slimed Sudoku.

Colouring Pens

CATCH THE SLIME

This is a fun activity to do with your friends and your favourite Slime!

You will need:

- [ ] A wire rack
- [ ] 4 glasses
- [ ] Drippy Slime
- [ ] 4 bowls
- [ ] A pair of scissors

Place tall glasses under your wire rack to raise it and place your bowls underneath.

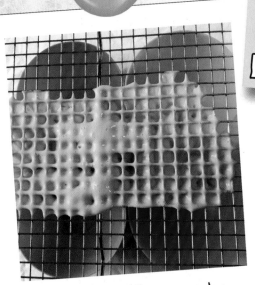

Spread the Slime on top of the rack and wait.

Just watch it ooze through the rack and try to catch it!

The Slime will slowly drip into the bowls!

For extra fun, snip the Slime with your scissors!

Which **tub** will catch the **most** Slime?

LEAD ME TO THE SLIME!

Which line will lead you to some Slime?

1 2 3 4

Answer on page **93**.

LAUGH OUT LOUD!

Why did the banana go to the hospital?

ANSWER: Because he wasn't peeling well!

MAGNETIC SLIME

You will need:

- [ ] 1 cup of PVA glue
- [ ] 1 tsp of bicarbonate of soda
- [ ] Food colouring (optional)
- [ ] 2 tsps of eyewash (must contain boric acid and sodium borate)
- [ ] Iron filings
- [ ] A magnet

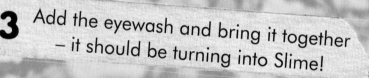

1 Combine the glue and the bicarbonate of soda – mix very well.

2 If you're using it, add the food colouring.

3 Add the eyewash and bring it together – it should be turning into Slime!

4 Now add the iron filings and mix well.

Vlog it!

This one would work well as a vlog!

5

Now take your magnet and hover it above your Slime. Move the magnet from side to side – does the Slime move too?

It's not magic...

...it's science!
The iron filings are attracted to the magnet and are trying to get to it through the Slime.

The GREAT SLIME Quiz!

1. If you put shaving foam in your Slime recipe what do you get?

2. What is a non-Newtonian fluid?

Shampoo

3. Can you make Slime with shampoo?

4. Is glue a polymer material?

5. If you add white vinegar to bicarbonate of soda what happens?

WHITE VINEGAR

6. Is water a monomer?

7. Is glue used to make printing inks?

8. What makes iron filings jump around?

9. Is Slime a liquid?

10. Is Slime a solid?

GLUE

Answers on page **93**.

RELEASE the SLIME!

START HERE

B U H R O E T C M O Q P I A U T V S E C H D O I Z E T R K O B D F G Z F K U S J M L S A I P X M E O N H T

Write down every third letter in the spaces and find out how to get the Slime tipped over.

Answer on page 93.

_ _ _ _ _ _ _ _ _ _ _ _ _ . _ _ _ _ _ _ _ _ _ _ _

I'd **love** that!

Choose a picture of a
lucky person and
stick it in. Slime them!

DREAM SLIME

1. If you could do whatever you wanted with Slime, what would it be?

2. Where would be the ultimate place to get Slimed?

3. What would be your secret Slime ingredient?

4. Who would be your ultimate person to Slime?

5. What would make the grossest Slime?

6. What would make the nicest Slime?

Shaken not Stirred SLIME!

You will need:

- [ ] An empty jam jar with a lid
- [ ] 240ml PVA glue
- [ ] 1 tsp bicarbonate of soda
- [ ] Food colouring (optional)
- [ ] 1 tbsp eyewash – it needs to have boric acid and sodium borate in it

You don't have to stir Slime to make it. Try this cool method and see if it's as good as stirring!

GLUE + +

2 Put in food colouring, if using.

1 Pour the glue into the jar with the bicarbonate of soda and mix well.

3 Add the eyewash.

4 Now screw the lid of the jar on tightly and shake.

5 Shake!

Use any container with a lid.

KEEP SHAKING! KEEP SHAKING! KEEP SHAKING!

6 Slime!

This makes a fun activity to do with your friends! Who can make Slime the fastest?

3... 2... 1... GO!

SLIME VLOG

Have you ever made a vlog?

Why not try one with our brilliant guide?

1 Decide what you want to vlog about. A Slime prank? A Slime recipe?

2 Set up your camera so it's ready to go.

If you are going to make Slime then gather all the ingredients together.

You could use:

☐ A camera

☐ A smartphone

☐ A tablet

GLUE

78

3 Work out the format of your blog – maybe have an introduction, then an activity and then a conclusion.

Introduction:
Say hello, who you are and what you're going to do in your vlog.

Activity:
Do your prank/recipe or activity – make sure you explain what you're doing.

Conclusion:
Let your viewers know how your activity has gone.

Goodbye:
Let your viewers know when they can expect to see you again and sign off.

4 Start filming – don't worry if it doesn't go according to plan, you can always edit stuff out.

TOP TIP

It can be nerve-wracking speaking to a camera. Try pretending that you're speaking to a close friend. Good luck!

5 Remember: be natural and be yourself!

6 Edit your video – if you need help then ask a grown-up.

Warning!
Make sure you ask an adult before filming and especially before publishing anything.

7 You're ready to publish!

Prank
SLIME JUICE

Follow the recipe to seriously gross out your thirsty friends!

You will need:
- [ ] A cup of water
- [ ] 1 tsp of fibre powder
- [ ] Food colouring – green might work best!

1 tsp 5 ml

1 Mix the water, fibre powder and food colouring together.

2 Next ask an adult to microwave it for one minute.

01:00

It should now have a Slimy consistency.

3 Now fill your drink carton with the **SLIME!**

OMG

4 Offer your friend a drink and pour the Slime juice into a glass for them

Make sure you ask a grown-up before doing this prank!

GROSS!

Warning! It won't taste nice but it's not dangerous to drink.

MORE PRANK JUICES

Add green food colouring to orange juice to change its colour and weird out your family.

YUCK!

SURPRISE!

Make up some strawberry jelly according to the packet instructions and pour it into drinking glasses. Chill them in the fridge until set and then offer them to your friends with a straw in.

Funny but delicious!

ULTIMATE SLIME

Which Slime suits you best?

1. When you make Slime, do you...

A: Like to add a sparkle?

B: Like to give it some volume?

C: Like to add something that will add a night-time vibe?

D: Like to add a surprise?

ABC or D?

2. You're pranking your bestie with Slime, do you...

A: Find their pencil case and put a picture of Slime in it?

B: Find something they are going to put their hand in and fill it to the top?

C: Wait until bedtime to try your joke?

D: They don't need to see this Slime, they can hear it coming!

ABC or D?

3. You'd like to make...

A: Something pretty.

B: Something cool.

C: Something for the dark.

D: Something out of the ordinary!

ABC or D?

4. You like to...

A: Shimmer like a star.

B: Find cute things to stroke.

C: Stand out from the crowd.

D: Be different!

ABC or D?

5. Your dream job would be...

A B C or D?

A: On stage.

B: Looking after animals.

C: In space.

D: A scientist.

6. Your most adventurous Slime was...

A B C or D?

A: Multicoloured!

B: So big!

C: Out of this world!

D: Full of weird stuff!

MAINLY A's
You're
Glittery Slime!

MAINLY C's
You're
Glow-in-the
-Dark Slime!

MAINLY B's
You're
Fluffy Slime!

MAINLY D's
You're
Popping Slime!

GLOW-IN-THE-DARK SLIME!

You will need:

- [ ] 1 cup of PVA glue
- [ ] 1 tsp bicarbonate of soda
- [ ] Glow powder
- [ ] 2 tbsp eyewash (must contain boric acid and sodium borate)

GLUE +

1 Mix the glue and bicarbonate of soda together.

2 Now add the glow powder.

3 Next add the eyewash and work it until you have your Slime consistency.

If you can't get hold of glow powder you can use glow sticks. Just place them in the Slime, and when the lights are off it will *glooowww!*

4 Turn off the lights!

Prank Time

Put a little in a jar in your bestie's bedroom. The next day, ask them how well they slept!

84

MATHS-A-GLOW-GLOW!

Try this crazy puzzle with glow sticks.

Move just one stick to make the sum work.

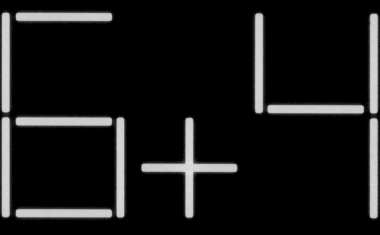 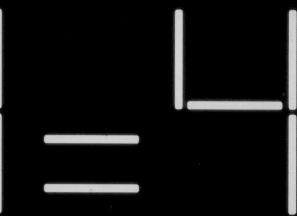

$$6 + 4 = 4$$

There are three possible answers! Can you get them all?

Answer 1.  8 - 4 = 4

Answer 2. 0 + 4 = 4

Answer 3. 5 + 4 = 9

Answers on page **93**.

See if you can figure out any other sums that would work in the same way!

Your reward? Slime heaven!

WHAT'S YOUR SLIME! NAME?

Take the **first letter** of your first name and find it in the list. Your second name is always **SLIME**

First Name: *Super*

A = Super
B = Stinky
C = Crazy
D = Dream
E = Yummy
F = Awesome
G = Swamp
H = Amazing
I = Perfect
J = Sticky

K = Fun
L = Glitter
M = Fluffy
N = Prank
O = Cool
P = Party
Q = Power
R = Sublime
S = Rainbow
T = Sparkle

U = Fruity
V = Bubble
W = Gooey
X = Glow
Y = Best
Z = Silly

First Name: *Super* SLIME

Draw a picture of yourself as your Slime character. What would you wear? What would your hair be like?

JOKE TIME!

Knock, knock.
Whose there?
Slime.
Slime who?
Slime you!

What fruit is most like Slime?
Goo-seberries!

What's the slimiest dessert?
Key Slime pie

What did the baby Slime say?
Goo, goo!

What did one eye say to the other eye?
Don't look now but something between us smells.

Why can't you trust atoms?
They make up everything.

Why do kids love Slime jokes?
Because they are goo-rate!

What did the Slime say when he ran out of time?
How Slime flies!

What do you do with blue Slime?
Cheer it up!

What do you say to someone up to their neck in Slime?
Not enough Slime!

What do you think of this book?
It's Slime-sational!

LAUGH OUT LOUD!

These jokes are hilarious! Can you make some up yourself?

1.

2.

YOUR PERFECT SLIME!

Pick and mix these ingredients to make your perfect personalised Slime.

Use the letters from your name to pick the ingredients out.

A = ☑ Glitter

B = ☐ Fluffy

C = ☐ Sand

D = ☑ Glow

E = ☑ Popping candy

F = ☐ Green colour

G = ☐ Pom poms

H = ☐ Plastic animals

I = ☑ Red colour

J = ☐ Glitter strands

K = ☐ Marbles

L = ☐ Blue colour

M = ☐ Eyeballs

N = ☑ Iron shavings

O = ☐ Lavender oil

P = ☐ Yellow colour

Q = ☐ Straw

R = ☐ Gold paint

S = ☑ Almond essence

T = ☐ Black colour

U = ☐ Oregano (herb)

V = ☐ Silver paint

W = ☐ Mint flavour

X = ☐ Beads

Y = ☑ Glitter glue

Z = ☐ Gems

MY PERFECT SLIME HAS:

- Glitter
- Glow x2
- Red coulor

- Almond essence
- Glitter glue
- Iron shavings

Of course you could always make up a name if you want a certain ingredient and your name doesn't get it for you!

Answers

Page 9 – Historical Slime
The word Slime appears **11** times.

Page 13 – More Slime! Wordsearch
The word Slime appears **17** times.

Page 27 – Slime! Anagrams
mile, me, lime, slim, lie, smile, elm, semi, is, sim

Page 38 – Fluffy Slime! Codebreaker
Shaving Foam

Page 47 – Slime Sequences

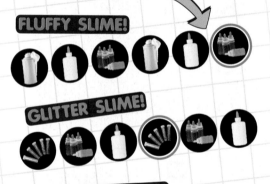

Page 46 – Underground Maze

P50–51 – Find the Slime

The Slime coordinates are **P,6**

Page 53 – Spot the Difference

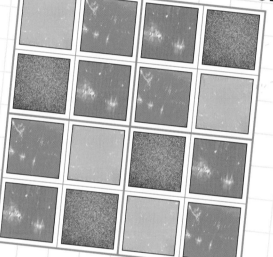

Page 65 – Slimed Sudoku!

Page 67 – Lead me to the Slime!

Number 3

Page 70–71 – The Great Slime Quiz!

1. Fluffy Slime
2. Neither a solid nor a liquid
3. Yes, just add salt!
4. Yes, glue is a polymer
5. It explodes!
6. Yes, water is a monomer
7. Yes, glue is used to make printing inks
8. A magnet
9. Slime is not a liquid
10. Slime is not a solid

Page 72–73 – Release the Slime!

Push it off, Slime them!

Page 85 – Maths-a-Glow-Glow!

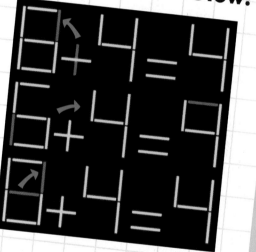